# SEPARATE IS NEVER EQUAL

## Sylvia Mendez & Her Family's Fight for Desegregation

# DUNCAN TONATIUH

ABRAMS BOOKS FOR YOUNG READERS · NEW YORK

SYLVIA HAD ON HER BLACK SHOES. They were shiny-new. Her hair was perfectly parted in two long *trenzas*. It was her first day at the Westminster school. The halls were crowded with students. She was looking for her locker when a young white boy pointed at her and yelled, "Go back to the Mexican school! You don't belong here!"

For the rest of the day, Sylvia did not speak or introduce herself in her classes. She kept her head down when walking in the halls. When she got home that afternoon, she told her mom, Felícitas, what had happened. "I don't want to go to that school anymore. The kids are mean."

"Sylvia," said her mother. *"¿No sabes que por eso luchamos?"* "Don't you know that is why we fought?"

Three years earlier, in the summer of 1944, Sylvia and her brothers, Jerome and Gonzalo Jr., and their parents had moved from the crowded city of Santa Ana, California, to a farm in nearby Westminster. Her father, Gonzalo Mendez, had labored for years as a field-worker, picking grapes and oranges. Now he was leasing a farm. He was going to be the boss. On their new farm they were going to grow asparagus, chilies, and tomatoes.

As the summer came to an end and the first day of school neared, Aunt Soledad drove Sylvia and her brothers and their cousins, Alice and Virginia, to the local public school on 17th Street so they could enroll. Sylvia was going to enter third grade. Gonzalo was going to enter second, and Jerome first.

*What a handsome building,* thought Sylvia as they pulled into the parking lot. Tall trees lined the street in front of the school. There was a playground with monkey bars and a red swing. When they walked into the school, they noticed that the hallways were spacious and clean.

"I'm here to enroll the children in school," said Aunt Soledad when they arrived at the principal's office.

The secretary gave Aunt Soledad two enrollment forms, one for Alice and one for Virginia. But she did not give her enrollment forms for Sylvia and her brothers.

"They cannot attend this school," said the secretary. "They must go to the Mexican school."

*Why do I have to go to the Mexican school?* Sylvia wondered. She was not Mexican—she was American. She spoke perfect English. Her father was from Mexico, but he had become a U.S. citizen. Her mother was from Puerto Rico, which was a U.S. territory.

Aunt Soledad was upset. "But we all live in this part of town!"

Sylvia looked at her cousins. They had light skin and long auburn hair, and their last name was Vidaurri—their father was Mexican, but of French descent. Then she looked at her brothers, and at her own hands and bare arms. She wondered, *Is it because we have brown skin and thick black hair and our last name is Mendez?*

"Rules are rules," said the secretary. "The Mendez children have to go to the Mexican school."

"I will not be enrolling any of them, then," said Aunt Soledad, and she stormed out of the office, taking Sylvia and the other children with her.

When they arrived home, Aunt Soledad told Sylvia's father what had happened. Mr. Mendez told her not to worry—it had to be a mistake. He would take care of it. He was a businessman, and he was used to dealing with people.

The next day, Mr. Mendez met with Mr. Harris, the superintendent of the Westminster school. Mr. Mendez explained that his family had just moved to a nearby farm. "The public school on 17th Street is the closest school to our house, and my children should attend it."

"Your children have to go to the Mexican school," said Mr. Harris.

"But why?" asked Mr. Mendez.

He was not given an answer other than, "That is how it is done."

In the following days, Mr. Mendez met with Mr. Atkinson, the county superintendent—Mr. Harris's superior—and then with the school board, which oversaw all of the schools in Orange County. But they all said the same thing: "Your children have to go to the Mexican school."

"But why?" Mr. Mendez kept asking.

No one would give him a satisfactory answer.

That fall, Sylvia and her brothers had to attend Hoover Elementary, better known as "the Mexican school," on Olive Street in the city of Westminster.

The building was a clapboard shack, and the halls were not spacious or clean. A cow pasture surrounded the school. The students had to eat their lunch outside, and flies would land on their food. There was an electric wire that surrounded the pasture to keep the cows in. If you touched it, you received a shock! The school did not have a playground—not even a swing.

The Mendez family did not give up. Time and time again, Sylvia heard her father talk with coworkers, friends, and other parents. "It's not fair that our kids have to go to an inferior school," he said. "It's not only the building that's a problem—the teachers at the school don't care about our children's education. They expect them to drop out by the eighth grade. How will our children succeed and become doctors, lawyers, or teachers?"

Mr. Mendez created a group called the Parents' Association of Mexican-American Children. He tried to collect signatures for a petition to integrate schools so that all children, regardless of their skin color or background, could have the same opportunities. But every time he asked someone to sign the petition, he would get the same answer. *"No queremos problemas."* "We don't want any problems." Many of the parents worked on farms owned by white families and feared they would lose their jobs if they supported the petition.

One day, a truck driver overheard Mr. Mendez trying to convince a worker to sign his petition. "You know," said the truck driver, "you could file a lawsuit."

The truck driver told Mr. Mendez about a lawyer named David Marcus, who had filed a lawsuit on behalf of people in San Bernardino and had helped them integrate the public pools there. At that time, not only were schools segregated but also other public places as well, such as pools, parks, and movie theaters. Some businesses even had signs that read, NO DOGS OR MEXICANS ALLOWED.

Mr. Mendez decided right then and there to hire Mr. Marcus, even if it meant having to spend all of his savings to do so.

NO DOGS or MEXICANS ALLOWED
—
PUBLIC POOL

Over the next few months, Mr. Mendez and Mr. Marcus traveled all over Orange County looking for people who had experienced similar problems.

Sylvia watched her father leave early in the morning. Sometimes she saw him come home in the evening, but often she only heard his footsteps when he got in late at night.

While he was away, Sylvia's mother had to take care of the farm. Mrs. Mendez would get Sylvia and her brothers ready for school, and then she would go out to the fields. She started the irrigation system, drove the tractor, oversaw the workers, and solved any problems that arose.

With the help of Mr. Marcus, Mr. Mendez found and talked with other families who were dealing with segregation. One of them was the Estrada family. Mr. Estrada had fought in World War II. He had risked his life next to Americans of all races and backgrounds. But when he returned to America from the war, he found out that his children were not allowed to attend school with white children. *"Es una injusticia,"* said Mr. Mendez. "It's an injustice."

The Estrada family joined the Mendez case, and so did three more families. The families were from the different school districts in Orange County: Westminster (where Sylvia lived), Garden Grove, El Modena, and Santa Ana. Mr. Marcus wanted to show that the segregation of students affected not only Sylvia and her brothers but more than five thousand children in the public school system all over Orange County.

On March 2, 1945, Mr. Marcus went to the courthouse and filed the lawsuit.

The trial was held at a courthouse in Los Angeles. Sylvia and her family dressed in their best clothes and sat in the courtroom to listen. The hearing lasted five days. Each day, Mr. Marcus called to the stand parents from the different districts in Orange County, and the superintendents from each district too.

On the first day, Mr. Kent, the superintendent of the Garden Grove district, was questioned. He said that he sent children to the Mexican school to help them improve their English.

*That is a lie!* thought Sylvia. Her English was as good as the English of any of the children at the Westminster school.

"Do you give the children any tests?" asked Mr. Marcus.

Mr. Kent claimed he did. "We do so by talking to them."

*That is another lie!* Sylvia wanted to yell. No one had questioned her. They rejected her from the Westminster school without asking her a thing.

"For what other reasons do you send children to the Mexican school?" asked Mr. Marcus.

Sylvia and her family braced themselves to hear what Mr. Kent would say next.

"For their social behavior. They need to learn cleanliness of mind, manner, and dress. They are not learning that at home. They have problems with lice, impetigo, and tuberculosis. They have generally dirty hands, face, neck, and ears."

The Mendez family and others in the room stared at Mr. Kent in disbelief. What he was saying was not true! It was degrading.

"How many of the two hundred ninety-two children at the Mexican school are inferior to whites in personal hygiene?" asked Mr. Marcus.

"At least seventy-five percent."

"And in their scholastic ability?"

"Seventy-five percent."

"In what other respects are they inferior?"

"In their economic outlook, in their clothing, and in their ability to take part in the activities of the school."

"Do you believe that white students are superior to Mexicans in the respects that you have mentioned?"

"Yes."

"And is that one of the reasons they are being segregated?"

"Yes."

Time and again, Mr. Mendez had asked, "Why can't my children attend the Westminster school?" Now he had his answer.

On the second day, Mr. Marcus called to the stand a fourteen-year-old student from the Mexican school in El Modena. Her name was Carol Torres. She spoke perfect English. It was clear that she had not been sent to the Mexican school because she had problems speaking the language, as the defense lawyers claimed.

Mr. and Mrs. Mendez were questioned on the third and fourth day, and so was Mr. Harris, the superintendent of the Westminster school. Sylvia was not called to the stand, but she was ready to testify if they asked her to. She tried

looking her best every morning, and she practiced what she would answer.

On the fifth and final day of the hearing, Mr. Marcus called to the stand two education specialists to explain why it was bad to segregate children into different schools. "Segregation tends to give an aura of inferiority. In order to have the people of the United States understand one another it is necessary for them to live together, and the public school is the one mechanism where all the children of all the people go," said one of them.

The judge nodded his head. He seemed to agree with this.

Judge Paul McCormick took almost a year to give his decision . . . but when he did, he ruled in favor of the Mendez family! In his ruling, he said that "public education must be open to all children by unified school association regardless of lineage." This meant that everyone must be allowed to attend school, no matter what his or her race or background.

The Mendez victory made newspaper headlines. Sylvia's family was ecstatic. But they did not have much time to celebrate because the school board appealed and asked a different court to review the case and the judge's decision. The case was reviewed by the appeals court in San Francisco in Northern California.

The Mendez family received support from the League of United Latin American Citizens, the National Association for the Advancement of Colored People, the Japanese American Citizens League, the American Jewish Congress, and other organizations. These groups sent letters with information relevant to the case and asked the judge to rule in favor of the Mendez family.

Sylvia was amazed that people of different backgrounds and from different parts of the country who had never met her family were getting involved in the

case and trying to help them. But her mother said, "*Cuando la causa es justa, los demás te siguen.*" "When you fight for justice, others will follow."

On April 15, 1947, the judges in the Court of Appeals in San Francisco ruled in favor of the Mendez family again.

That June, Governor Earl Warren signed the law that said that all children in California were allowed to go to school together, regardless of race, ethnicity, or language.

"So, remember," said Sylvia's mother, "we fought to make sure you could attend a good school and have equal opportunities."

Sylvia thought long and hard about what her mother said. The next day, she returned to the Westminster school. This time she did not listen to any whispers. She ignored the children who pointed at her and called her names. Instead, she held her head high. Her parents had fought not only for her and her brothers but for all their classmates.

Looking around, she saw that other children were smiling at her. By the end of the day, she had made a friend. And by the end of the school year, she had made many friends of different backgrounds. She knew that her family had fought for that.

# AUTHOR'S NOTE

In the 1940s, segregation based on race or national origin was common throughout the United States. The *Mendez* v. *Westminster School District* case paved the way for the desegregation of schools in America. After the Mendez lawsuit, similar suits were filed and won in Texas and Arizona. In 1954, seven years after the Mendez victory, the landmark case *Brown* v. *Board of Education* desegregated schools in the entire country.

Two people who played key roles in the *Brown* case had also been involved in the *Mendez* case: Thurgood Marshall and Earl Warren. As a member of the National Association for the Advancement of Colored People, Marshall had sent friend-of-the-court briefs to the judge in the *Mendez* case. In these letters he argued against segregation. He later used several of the same arguments when he became the lawyer in the *Brown* case. Earl Warren was the governor who signed into law the desegregation of schools in California after the Mendez victory. He later became the chief justice of the U. S. Supreme Court. He presided over the *Brown* case and ruled in Brown's favor.

Sylvia (b. 1936) and her brothers attended the Westminster school until her family moved back to Santa Ana. Sylvia graduated from an integrated high school and attended California State University, where she studied to become a registered nurse. She worked for thirty-three years at a medical center in Los Angeles and then retired to take care of her ill mother. Sylvia remembers that before Felícitas passed away, she regretted the fact that so few people knew about the *Mendez* case and her family's fight for equality. Indeed, the *Mendez* case is seldom taught in schools. Unlike *Brown* v. *Board of Education*, which is widely known, *Mendez* v. *Westminster* is known by few Americans to this day. After her mother died, Sylvia made it her mission to educate people about her family's fight for desegregation.

In recent decades, the *Mendez* case has finally begun to receive some attention and recognition. Documentaries have been made about it, and books and articles have been written about it. In 2002, a public school in Santa Ana was named after Felícitas and Gonzalo Mendez. In 2007, a commemorative stamp was issued by the U.S. Postal Service to celebrate the fiftieth anniversary of the Mendez victory. In 2009, a high school in Los Angeles was named the Felícitas and Gonzalo Mendez Learning Center. And in 2011, Sylvia Mendez received the Presidential Medal of Freedom from President Barack Obama. It is the highest civilian award a person can receive in America.

Thanks to the efforts of courageous people like the Mendez family, the segregation of public schools is illegal in the United States. Unfortunately, a great deal of inequality—and a kind of unofficial segregation—still exists today.

According to a 2012 study by the Civil Rights Project at the University of California, Los Angeles, across the United States segregation has increased significantly in recent years. It reported that 43 percent of Latino students and 38 percent of black students attend schools where fewer than 10 percent of their classmates are white. The study, which analyzes data from the Department of Education, also reveals that Latino and black children are twice as likely to be in school where the majority of students are poor. Therefore, their schools are likely to have fewer resources and less experienced teachers. All too often I see this inequality when I visit schools in different parts of the country to read and to talk about my books.

The Mendez family went to court almost seventy years ago, but their fight is relevant today. As the education specialists in the trial argued, the segregation of children creates feelings of superiority in one group and inferiority in another. We need to be able to interact and mingle so that prejudices break down, so that we can learn from one another, and so that everyone has a fair shot at success.

My hope is that this book will help children and young people learn about this important yet little known event in American history. I also hope that they will see themselves reflected in Sylvia's story and realize that their voices are valuable and that they too can make meaningful contributions to this country.

*Top left:* Sylvia as a young girl, 1947. *Top right:* Sylvia in 2011, after receiving the Presidential Medal of Freedom. *Bottom left:* Sylvia's parents, 1947. *Middle right:* The Westminster school. *Bottom right:* Hoover Elementary.

# GLOSSARY

**American Jewish Congress:** an association that promotes Jewish interests in the United States and other countries

**appeal:** to request, after a trial is finished, that a higher court review the outcome

**brief:** a legal term that refers to a summary prepared for a lawyer at a trial

**case:** a dispute between opposing parties, resolved by a court

**citizen:** a person who owes allegiance to the government and is entitled to full civic rights and privileges

**court:** a judge or a judicial body that makes decisions in cases according to the law

**courthouse:** a building where a case is tried

**court of appeals:** a court that reviews decisions made by lower courts

**courtroom:** a room within a courthouse where a case is tried

**decision:** a judge's conclusion after hearing both sides of a case; a ruling

**degrading:** causing a loss of self-respect

**equal opportunity:** a policy of treating others without discrimination, especially on the basis of their gender, race, or age

**ethnicity:** a group of people who have a common national or cultural tradition

**field-worker:** an agricultural laborer, often working long hours for low pay

**hygiene:** conditions relating to health, especially personal well-being

**impetigo:** a skin disease

**inferior:** of lesser quality

**injustice:** something that is not fair

**integrate:** to open to members of all races, ethnicities, and other groups

**Japanese American Citizens League:** an association that protects civil and human rights and works for social change, particularly in the Asian–Pacific American community

**judge:** a public official, appointed or elected, who oversees cases in a court

**lawsuit:** a dispute brought to a court for a decision to be made; a case

**lawyer:** a person educated in the law who advises others on legal matters

**League of United Latin American Citizens:** the largest Latino civil rights organization in the United States

**National Association for the Advancement of Colored People:** an association that works for equal rights and to eliminate racial discrimination

**opportunity:** a chance to advance

**petition:** a formal written document requesting a right or benefit from a person or group in authority

**public school:** a school paid for by public funds that provides free education to the children of a community or district

**rule:** to decide; to issue a ruling

**ruling:** a court decision

**school board:** a group of public officials that oversees public schools in a defined area

**school district:** an area, such as a neighborhood, town, or county, whose public schools are administered together

**segregate:** to separate people based on race, ethnicity, class, or other factors

**"separate but equal":** a policy based on the U.S. Supreme Court ruling in *Plessy v. Ferguson* (1896) that holds that certain groups of people can be denied access to public spaces, such as schools, housing, eating establishments, restrooms, pools, and entertainment facilities, as long as they are provided facilities of an equal nature

**stand:** the place in a courtroom where a witness sits (or stands) while being questioned by a lawyer

**superintendent:** the head of a school district. States define the role and authority of a school superintendent in different ways.

**superior:** of greater quality

*trenza:* a hair braid

**trial:** a formal examination of evidence by a judge or jury, in order to make a decision in a case

**tuberculosis:** a potentially fatal disease of the lungs

**U.S. territory:** an area, such as Puerto Rico, that is governed by the United States but is not a state

# BIBLIOGRAPHY

**Interviews**
Author interviews with Sylvia Mendez in Austin, Texas, October 2012, and in Fullerton, California, April 2013.

**Transcripts**
Documents and records of *Mendez v. Westminster* (1946) can be found at the National Archives at Riverside (Perris, Calif.). Documents and records of *Mendez v. Westminster* (1947) can be found at the National Archives at San Francisco (Bruno, Calif.). For information on the National Archives and Record Administration, go to http://www.archives.gov/research.

**Films**
Bennett, Erica, and Fred Paskiewicz. *Mendez v. Westminster: Families for Equality.* Fullerton, Calif.: Fullerton College, 2010.
Robbie, Sandra. *Mendez vs. Westminster: For All the Children/Para todos los niños.* Huntington Beach, Calif.: KOCE-TV, 2002.

**Books**
Conkling, Winifred. *Sylvia and Aki.* Berkeley, Calif.: Tricycle Press, 2011.
Matsuda, Michael, and Sandra Robbie. *Los Méndez contra la ciudad de Westminster: Por todos los niños; La historia de una victoria de derechos civiles en los Estados Unidos.* Yorba Linda, Calif.: Blue State Press, 2006.
Strum, Philippa. *Mendez v. Westminster: School Desegregation and Mexican-American Rights.* Lawrence, Kans.: University Press of Kansas, 2010.

**Articles and Reports**
Arriola, Christopher. "Knocking on the Schoolhouse Door: Mendez v. Westminster, Equal Protection, Public Education, and Mexican Americans in the 1940's." La Raza Law Journal 8, no. 2 (1995).
Civil Rights Project at the University of California, Los Angeles. *"E Pluribus . . . Separation: Deepening Double Segregation for More Students."* http://civilrightsproject.ucla.edu/research/k-12-education/integration-and-diversity/mlk-national/e-pluribus...separation-deepening-double-segregation-for-more-students. Accessed August 21, 2013.
Luhby, Tami. "Worsening Wealth Inequality by Race." CNN Money, June 21, 2012. http://money.cnn.com/2012/06/21/news/economy/wealth-gap-race/index.htm. Accessed July 19, 2013.
Orfield, Gary, John Kucsera, and Genevieve Siegel-Hawley. *"E Pluribus . . . Separation: Deepening Double Segregation for More Students."* Report of the Civil Rights Project, University of California, Los Angeles, 2012.
Rich, Motoko. "Segregation Prominent in Schools, Study Finds." New York Times, September 19, 2012. http://www.nytimes.com/2012/09/20/education/segregation-prominent-in-schools-study-finds.html. Accessed August 21, 2013.

Ruiz, Vicki L. "We Always Tell Our Children They Are Americans: *Mendez v. Westminster* and the California Road to *Brown v. Board of Education.*" *College Board Review* no. 200 (Fall 2003): 20–27.

**Websites**
"Before *Brown v. Board of Education*," on National Public Radio website: http://www.npr.org/templates/story/story.php?storyId=1784243.
*Mendez v. Westminster Case:* www.mendezwestminstercase.blogspot.com.
Sylvia and Sandra Mendez Duran's page on StoryCorps website: http://storycorps.org/listen/sylvia-mendez-and-sandra-mendez-duran/.
Sylvia Mendez's personal site: http://sylviamendezinthemendezvswestminster.com.
"2010 Presidential Medal of Freedom Recipient—Sylvia Mendez," on White House website: http://www.whitehouse.gov/photos-and-video/video/2011/02/16/2010-presidential-medal-freedom-recipient-sylvia-mendez.

# ABOUT THE TEXT

The dialogue in the trial scene comes directly from court transcripts. I shortened and edited it for clarity and pacing. The dialogue in the rest of the book is inspired by conversations I had with Sylvia Mendez in October 2012 and April 2013.

# INDEX

TO THE MEMORY OF GONZALO AND FELÍCITAS MENDEZ
AND TO PATTY, FOR ALL HER LOVE AND SUPPORT
—D.T.

The illustrations for this book were hand-drawn and then collaged and colored digitally.

Cataloging-in-Publication Data has been applied for and may be obtained from the Library of Congress.
ISBN: 978-1-4197-1054-4

Text copyright © 2014 Duncan Tonatiuh
Illustrations copyright © 2014 Duncan Tonatiuh
Book design by Maria T. Middleton

Printed and bound in U.S.A.
16 15 14 13 12 11 10

Abrams Books for Young Readers are available at special discounts when purchased in quantity for premiums and promotions as well as fundraising or educational use. Special editions can also be created to specification. For details, contact specialsales@abramsbooks.com or the address below.

ABRAMS The Art of Books
115 West 18th Street, New York, NY 10011
abramsbooks.com